# THE BUSHMAN'S MEDICINE SHOW

OTHER BOOKS *by* GARY COPELAND LILLEY

*High Water Everywhere* (Willow Books, 2013)

*Cape Fear* (Q Ave Press, 2012)

*Alpha Zulu* (Ausable Press, 2008)

*Black Poem* (Hollyridge Press, 2005)

*The Reprehensibles* (Fractal Edge Press, 2004)

*The Subsequent Blues* (Four Way Books, 2004)

# THE BUSHMAN'S
# MEDICINE SHOW

*poems*
## Gary Copeland Lilley

LOST HORSE PRESS
Sandpoint, Idaho

# ACKNOWLEDGMENTS

Grateful acknowledgment if made to the journals in which these poems first appeared:

*Best American Poetry 2014:* "Sermon of the Dreadnaught"
*MiPoesias:* "Sermon of the Dreadnaught"
*Taos International Journal of Poetry:* "Working with Rednecks: Part 2"
*The Bark:* "Tobacco Road"
*Waxwing:* "I Told You" and "Meet Me in the Bottom"
*Willow Springs:* "A Proper Elegy for My Father" and "Tobacco Road"


To my brother, Bradford, and his wife Ernestine, for anchoring my boat-adrift soul to Carolina, and to the Norfleet Family for listening to and passing on the cobalt-blue bejeweled words of our ancestors.

To the many friends that I have made music with, including Ahmad Baabahar, Kim Addonizio, Sam Ligon, Terry Harmonica Bean, Matt Sircely, Guy Davis, Blackheart, the Riddick Grove Missionary Baptist Church Choir, Valerie and Ben Turner, Cornelius Eady, and my *Noff Cackalack* band members Ryan Wensil and Chris Feathers.

I am so beholden to you all.

*Cover Art:* Christine Holbert.
*Author Photo:* Mike McAndrews, Port Townsend, Washington.
*Book & Cover Design:* Christine Holbert.

FIRST EDITION

This and other LOST HORSE PRESS titles may be viewed online at www.losthorsepress.org.

LIBRARY OF CONGRESS CATALOGING-IN-PUBLICATION DATA

Names: Lilley, Gary, author.
Title: The Bushman's medicine show : poems / Gary Copeland Lilley.
Description: First edition. | Sandpoint, Idaho : Lost Horse Press, [2017]
Identifiers: LCCN 2016051838 | ISBN 9780996858496 (trade pbk. : alk. paper)
Classification: LCC PS3612.I42 A6 2017 | DDC 811/.6—dc23
LC record available at https://lccn.loc.gov/2016051838

# CONTENTS

*The Bushman's Medicine Show*

1 Standing on the Corner When Being Cool Went Blind

2 Back When I Knew Betty Boop

3 The Prayer That Is in My Blood

6 Two Trains Running 1

7 Two Trains Running 2

8 What King Elijah Told Me Happened to Robert

10 Turned

12 Junior's Place: Holly Springs, Mississippi, 1997

13 Backslider

*The Bushman's Medicine Show*

17 The Haint Blue Bottle Tree

18 Tobacco Road

24 Working With Rednecks: Part One

25 Working With Rednecks: Part Two

27 The Grind

*The Bushman's Medicine Show*

31 Sermon of the Dreadnaught

33 On the Road to Blessing

34 Before the Bars Open

35 Before the Bars Close

36 In the Bar

37 After the Bar Closes

38 What Happens in the Mustang Stays in the Mustang

39 I Told You

*The Bushman's Medicine Show*

43  A Tuesday in the Crack War of '97
    1. Having Birthed a Holding Charge
    2. Going Solo
    3. Junieboy's Forty-Five:
    4. Black Flag
    5. Fish Bait
    6. Penitent at 2 AM in the Holding Cell

*The Bushman's Medicine Show*

51  Meet Me in the Bottom
53  The Wood
55  Domestic Violence
56  When My First Wife Left Me
58  Driving at Night Towards the Hood Canal
59  Ars Poetica
60  Simmer Down

*The Bushman's Medicine Show*

65  I Don't Believe in Levees
66  Asheville
68  The Boneyard
69  Isaac in the Shadow of Abraham
70  For Peace in the Valley
71  Love Poem: We Both Drink, Sometimes
72  My Sister's Raybans
73  A Proper Elegy for My Father

## The Bushman's Medicine Show

*Hold the water snakes*
*that hunt the creek in a moment*
*of abeyance, a submergence*
*of their natural demon selves.*

# STANDING ON THE CORNER
# WHEN BEING COOL WENT BLIND

*You've been slipping into darkness, whoa-whoa-whoa,*
*And pretty soon you're gonna pay.*

—War

Yeah baby, I'm the Bushman, everybody know me, a talking drum, I am the oral tradition, the griot of the cigarette. No bullshit. Ain't nothing but the truth, everything I tell you is airtight and waterproof. I can hoodoo and close view this neighborhood's future from the vantage of my stoop. Get down like I'm proud. I like mud-cloth so let that be my sanctified robe. Preach asked me what my religion was and I told him I channeled John Coltrane and became a devout musician. I always been a child of god, if you don't believe me just ask my blessed beloved mom. But tell me why do god's children have to experience every test? And exactly how much of a blessing comes with a financial offering? Well, consider the fact that all of our damned deeds need to be sermonized and somewhere deep in that sin darkness there's always a crack of light. It ain't for sale but nothing in this world is half-priced, and if what you end up with does not satisfy nobody's giving you that money back. Can you see me in that light, with the children of god, those blues people with the haints riding them hard. Please do tell all the other infidels that I believe the choruses falling out the mouths of the raggedy people that I'm around are the actual utterances of saints.

# BACK WHEN I KNEW BETTY BOOP

Before she found her woo-poo-pee-do
there was no guarantee of anything
after her come-up-and-see-me-sometime
straight whiskey talk or spending a night
touching those short black dreads a pagan
holistic hairdo drum the whatever dance
a rumor the please please please it's hot
standing beside her a tropical climate
New Orleans in August when the swamp heat
never leaves and she didn't like to be called
beautiful or hear the leer and compliment
on her body she hated such judgment
about the package she was in she was not
trying to pass and she really didn't care
to identify as white or negro for anybody's
benefit her hand went naturally to her hip
when walking that swag that signature slink.

# THE PRAYER THAT IS IN MY BLOOD

Let me see the sun slip
over the world in the morning.
I need to see God turn up the light.

I stood on the back porch
at night, smoked a cigar under
the holes that once held stars.

My five word prayer:
Lord, have mercy on me.

I need to find the old tree
with a hollow at the base,
and maybe with some roots exposed,
to place my offering.

Lucero the healer,
the wind the rain the storm,
are all in his beggar man hands,
he is the crossroad to my ancestors.

The uncles I never met.

George and Buddy, grandsons
of Jedidiah, avengers of my mother,
they are buried in Perquimans County
off Low Ground Road.

How do family deal with murder
when we have murdered?

Lord, have mercy on me.

What would make Lumbee Jim
attack my sixteen year old mother
before she became my mother?

What would make him come to the house
and kick in the door?

The eclipse is Lucero arriving,
messenger of God. The *muerto*
has come with him and now
walks with me.

There are things my mother never
talked about, I find my answers
in the cemetery. I need to see the sun
at the edge of the world.

Centella, my guide, leads me down
the line of family graves. I am steeped
in the manner which most of my people
worshiped, gave praise to the God
who delivered them from slavers to live
at the edge of the great dismal swamp.

Lucero, Centella, *muerto* and me:
kneeboning in the wilderness
a string of purple beads
at the tombstones of my folk.
Lord, have mercy on me.

I am born of drunken crime.

Lucero, the life-blood of justice,
integrity, the keeper of moral law.

Government law does not
always do what is right.

I hold down the anger,
keep the *muerto* in check.

Lucero makes things right.

I need to see that red glow
come over the horizon.

# TWO TRAINS RUNNING 1

Maybe I'm fool to want her like I do, after
walking away from woman, job, this town.

The leaving I've done, has anybody made more
small-headed mistakes when they were young?

The woman, the woman, the hauntingly right
woman; everything good was possible.

Something more than expected when coming
back home for this gig, but there she is.

Sitting in The Savoy Club, at the bar with a man
looking like he's two drinks from a fight.

Sometimes you got to be positive, and she
turns away like she was done with him.

I tip my hat, a soft pinch to the crown then slide
a finger across the brim, and she steps right up.

Tells me if I don't sing a song for her tonight
I'll never know the new tune she wants to play.

# TWO TRAINS RUNNING 2

I was just passing through and stopped at The Savoy,
and Joe Bottoms offers me a hundred dollars

to play two sets and there she was, looking very
late night, very early morning pretty, I'm a bad

situation that she knows too well because she met me
and been left two trips maybe three around the sun ago

and now she was at the bar with a frightening fella
drinking and peeping around his muscled neck

to see who wanted to mess with him, and yes,
I had that stainless steel pistol in my guitar case.

She slips a shoe, shows her toes, she was wearing
mules, size 7: can't no man hide a foot fetish.

She peeped me looking and ran her hand up
a smooth thigh, winked, and I go courageous,

put that steel pimp-flash pistol in my waist,
and cake walk over to buy her a drink.

## WHAT KING ELIJAH TOLD ME HAPPENED TO ROBERT

Eighteen months in prison with an assumed name
and a guitar, the only honest work he'd ever done

he liked to stand at the crossroads, the threshold
of his church and throw blues in four directions

when just past midnight the darkest man
he'd ever seen came up and tuned his Silvertone

somewhere in smoke from his dangling Lucky Strike
that cataract disappeared from his left eye

and from then on he could play anything scandalous
he wanted, and carried on with other men's wives

he knew how to smile and haunt the heart and leave
them bubbling a stew pot sitting on the stove

some young gal in every town he passed through
bought those jack-of-hearts suits he wore

he played his guitar like it was a woman and
turned his back if other bluesmen were watching

but the river floods every year like a covenant
and that week the promise of rain was in the air

the juke owner's wife was dressed up waiting
at the joint, pretty woman anticipating his wink

he had missed a swear of red dust when wiping
the Mississippi road from the shine of his shoes

the owner sent him a special bottle of hooch, and
when Johnny Shine tipped it over he asked for another

he was ripping through the songs just leering
at that woman, until he took sick and had to stop

in the small hours, towards the end, he was on all fours,
with the hellhounds growling in the dark

# TURNED

My twig-gathering landlord
(who lives directly below)
claims he was disturbed late
last night by my foot tapping
so I must have been listening
to music. He says he didn't hear
any music. But my tapping foot
was like some voodoo torture
that kept him up long after
it had stopped. Then he said
he heard me cooking four strips
of thick-sliced bacon, grits
and two brown eggs. I am
a county boy, but who does
he think he is; he just unchecked
northwest. He don't know I drove
the northern route across the country,
in the winter, and that I was once
four hundred miles west of nowhere
with less than enough cigarettes
to make it through the Badlands,
fire / brimstone gospel the only stations,
the hallelujah nation, on the radio.
He don't know I come from
the eat-a-chicken-wing-
down-to-the-bone people,
and I don't feel I have to tiptoe
around anything, but I longed
a peaceful place, so tonight
I housekeep my good friend's cabin
in the forest, and the firs, the madrones
and the willows, their bright green

tender leaf, the blooming bushes
I can't name, and dandelions
carpeting her yard, this is
the temporary paradise I need:
lazy-smoking a Spirit, coffee
an early dark morning, the blues
diminished moonlight,
a group of singing coyotes,
one loud hip-hopping frog
and no landlord.

## JUNIOR'S PLACE, HOLLY SPRINGS, MISSISSIPPI, 1997

Everyone in the Oxford bar told me,
don't get lost trying to find that juke,
it's dangerous. So I decided to avoid
making a wrong turn (how *many*
times do you get to do that without
it costing more than you care to pay,
because outside of Oxford didn't matter
what year it was I was still in Mississippi,
it has history). I would locate the juke
during day and go back that evening,
and I did find it, a clapboard shack
thrown beside a two-lane blacktop
and there wasn't anywhere to park
closer than a dark quarter-mile.
Tell you there's nothing bluer
than a Mississippi night on a road
splitting the woods, and an owl hoots
deep in the pines, the frogs croak
the probability and possibility of love,
this is what it means to be touched,
an ancestor spirit telling me I was in
the right place to find the folk,
my tribe of dancing moonshiners.
Closer to the juke the honeysuckle
in the treeline lingered, the stilled air,
perfume on a woman's wrist,
I could hear the teasing trance
of Junior's guitar over the drone
of the incessant crickets, and
as I approached the yard I could
hear the hill country soil
that I was dancing on.

## BACKSLIDER

My old man got up in Pastor Wiggins' face
at the meeting for the church's building fund
about awarding a contract to a non-local bidder,
and then challenged him to a fist fight after
the good Reverend prayed for the Lord to lend
the guiding hand and lead some of the men
of the congregation to give as much attention
to Sunday mornings as they give to the devil
every other day of the week, and my father
thought the Pastor was talking about him and
threatened to drag his ass off that pulpit
to get to the real deal in the church yard.

## The Bushman's Medicine Show

*I believe in everything
given in the word.
Trauma healing is what
I'm selling, a repair
to whatever damage
wraps around our bones.*

# THE HAINT BLUE BOTTLE TREE

For protecting the household
from evil spells and thieves
with invocations to your ancestors

create a bottle tree from one
growing in the yard, or build
the magic tree and place it

before the entrance to your home.
Your protection is in the power
of the dead, those from the other side

who work in the family's behalf.
Tie bottles to the branches, they reflect
the light you need, especially those

that are haint blue and contain
graveyard earth, to the branches
tie animal bones and stones.

The wicked will not prosper.
Whosoever dares to challenge
such protection will be laid bare,

and exposed for all to see.
Nothing good will be gained
by a thief on this property

except hoodoo justice, which
is swift and hovers now
just above their head.

# TOBACCO ROAD

## I.

I am fourteen, two years into my social isolation
after we moved from the grime and blacktop
basketball courts of my New York neighborhood
back to the piney woods and struggle farms,
into the grit of the North Carolina coastal plains.
I was the funny-talking city boy that every local boy
wanted to fight, until they accepted the fact
that I fight dirty. I would pick up anything,
maybe a smooth fist-size rock. Nobody wants
to get cracked 'side the head with that.
I spent summer mornings bare-chested, shirt tied
round my waist, running through the woods
with my dog, and if they were ripe, eating wild grapes
golden in the dappled shade, the vines hanging
from some low branch of a tree; running through
the deer beds, scaring up rabbits, and avoiding
the occasional snake or bear. Every day
my voice changing, back and forth, from a soft lilt
to the scratch inhabiting any song I try to sing.

## II.

Mr. Luther Grant
was coming through
the field between
our houses doing
his old pirate step.
His youngest brother
had chopped three toes
off that right foot
when he'd put it
on the block and dared
him to swing
the double-bladed ax.
I was peeling
potatoes on the porch
and when he saw
me he spit
the plug of tobacco
from his mouth
and the way
he set his jaw
indicated he had
something bad to say.

## III.

Queenie killed five of Mr. Luther Grant's chickens,
they say a dog that does that never stops.
She then laid herself among the dead birds,
surprised that they had stopped squawking, a game
of chase and catch where each chicken stopped
trying to fly away into the early afternoon heat.
She'd killed five in the treeless yard before she tired
of them and came back across the field, dropping
the last one halfway between the two houses.
I know Mr. Luther Grant had a right reason to be
upset; they say a dog that kills chicken never stops.
She was a city dog, my Uncle Willie's dog,
which he'd placed in my care after he was drafted
and knew he was going to Vietnam. His one
bedroom apartment had been Queenie's home.
She slept at the foot of his bed and they went
on daily runs in the park. When Willie gave his dog to me
I'd begged my father not to put her on the chain.
One of the few times I've seen him agree to anything
that wasn't his idea. And now, my dog Queenie
killed five of Luther Grant's egg-laying chickens,
and they say a dog that does that won't ever stop.

## IV.

My father was drinking in the kitchen while
reading his Bible. He comes out, and greets
Luther Grant in the yard. They purposely
keep their eyes off me but are talking loud
enough to ensure that I can hear them. They are
formally polite. My mother washing dishes, watches
everything through the kitchen window and
looks her sorrow down on me and begins
a hymnal song, *You'll Understand It Better
Bye and Bye*. Queenie, on the porch panting
in the late afternoon corner of shade is not allowed
in the house. My mother says all animals belong
outside. She dries her hands with the dish towel,
drapes the soft cloth on the kitchen sink.

# V.

My mother steps out on the tilting porch,
*Let me help you peel those taters.*

We sit together on the glide and work silently.
A crow lights on the willow near the porch and calls.

Queenie perks her ears, waiting to see if it would
come to ground. I am glad that it does not.

Mr. Grant stops talking, pulls out his chaw, and turns
to leave. My father promises to take care of it.

## VI.

We are in the woods and the sun
is shining on the loblolly pines,
twilight a hint in the near distance.
Not a cloud in the Carolina sky.
We pass a tree of wild golden grapes,
the vines hanging heavy off the low branches.
Flirting birds chatter at the abundance.
My father walks a quick-step ahead
while my dog trots beside me, he has
ordered me to come along, but I refuse
to carry the shovel or the loaded gun.

# WORKING WITH REDNECKS: PART ONE

Like looking through a binocular backwards
the green fields of young feed corn
seemed to have furrows a mile long
rolling past the curved horizon of the world.
There were two-hundred rich acres and not
a shade tree on it. July in the Carolinas,
the impenitent heat rising like a scrim,
putting the shimmer in the far-off forest.
In the peak of the exposed afternoon
while chopping the weeds around the corn,
or riding in the steel beds of the trucks
and on the steel saddles of the tractors,
sweating through the long sleeves
and heavy jeans: some days you eat the bear,
but on these kinds of days the bear eats you.
The white bosses driving the pick-ups
know it, and their Cola drinking sons riding
beside them in their aviator shades and shorts
and fertilizer ballcaps, they know it.
And all the hands from Sandy Cross know it, too.
There is one bent and dented metal dipper;
all the hands pass it along drinking
the agreed upon two full dippers from
the diminishing orange cooler in the back
of one of the trucks. This time of day the ice
long been gone and you smell hot plastic
like it's some bad medicine in the water.

# WORKING WITH REDNECKS: PART TWO

The white bosses and their sons on
the long steps of the store's porch,
the men drinking Buds while their boys
drank red cans of cold Colas. I wanted one,
strolled into the store like I was back in
New York, and all the hands followed me
to the counter where I pull out a sweated
dollar and lay it down for a cold soda.
A white man, in a white KKK tee-shirt,
looked at me like he barely could see me,
then he slowly reached into the chest freezer
and got me a cold Cola. All the hands
bought one, and we walked back to sit
in the shade on crates and buckets under
the roof over the gasoline pumps, talking
on each other's sisters when the white boys
get up, and one of them about my age of 15
crushed his empty can and threw it at me.
I threw it back, hitting him side the head,
knocking aviator shades into Carolina dirt
in front of the white bosses, the white bosses
all stood up, and one of them, Jasper Edmond,
said "Go to him Junior, don't you ever take shit
from a nigger." The hands got up, moved away,
and Junior came at me. Scared, very white.
My first blow, in the middle of his face
and he went down blowing blood from
his broken nose, then looked back at his
fat father. He got up and came again, slow,
ready to stop if he could find a white way
to do so, but I had bear funk on me, I hit him
and he's on all fours, blood-mouthing

the word please. I stepped back and walked
saying I quit, looking at his fat-ass father,
who said that he was gonna surely pay me
what I goddamn had coming for the day.
I told him you can keep whatever
you want to pay, this was free.

## THE GRIND

A bleak Saturday, a January morning
with the promise of ice and snow,
I walked to the truck to my father,
his Marlboros glare and glower at me
because I'd come home drunk
and stinking the night before
the hog killing.

I know you can't come home
from a juke joint drunk
when you have to be up 'fore sunrise
to build the fire that heats
the water that scalds the dead hog
for the scrapers.

The old man guns the motor to say
I'm moving too slow
still pissed because I jumped in
when he jumped on my mother
for complaining about his gambling debts
even though I agree with him
that every poor boy is entitled
to take a chance on luck.

Same as me when I go to the juke joint.
If Doris Hunter is going to be there
dancing in her "my everything" dress
no matter how cold it is outside
everybody in the joint
is going to be sweating.

Nobody boogaloos quite
like Doris who kissed me
after a homecoming game.
I was the score the picked off pass
crisscross the field.
My father never once saw me play
he does not claim me
as his own it seems colder
in the truck than in the yard
of brown frozen weeds.

There is just a crack of sunlight
rising above the tree line
the edge of the field the temperature
seems to be dropping
a small bullet a big hog
shot right between the eyes.

The Carolina winter never relents
never gives me comfort. I knew
when I stepped out the house
I was not dressed warm enough
no protection from the cold front
but I didn't go back to get the heavier coat
because who the hell wants to hear
the ugly, to hear all that nasty lip.

### The Bushman's Medicine Show

*In the beginning word was god,*
*and the music thereof. The spirit*
*is in the laundromat, the washers*
*humming as I fold work clothes*
*from the dryer. What else have we*
*ever had that was stronger*
*than a mojo rising, stronger*
*than our faith? The thin pages all*
*speak of it being heard and seen.*

# SERMON OF THE DREADNAUGHT

The guitar: I take communion
daily in this shack of a church

with a moaners' bench rubbed
smooth by repentant backsliders.

I listen to the seventh note,
graced by God, it is my battle-ax,

a joyful noise no more modern
than that old-time religion

cooking on the woodstove
in my grandmother's kitchens.

Holy ghosted, I have been washed
in the blackwater cypress swamp

that flows inside my guitar.
A solid top, and I play it righteous

as any stingy brim disciple that ever
has played a small town bus-stop,

and I got a missing canine tooth
from the right side of my mouth

and now my gospel is cobalt blue.
I remember the purity of the old guys,

Lucky Strike smokers and homebrew
drinkers with open tunings, sanctified

imperfections, scarred and battered
harmonies. They have introduced me

to the hollering haints who hold
late night prayer service in my guitar.

I believe in the palm oil that anoints
the guitar. I believe in life as sure

as I believe in death. I confess
the ancestor spirits and their love

accompanies me. The bloodline
has dressed me in that glorious suit

that we only wear when we are
our true selves. In the ascending heat

there is a train of guitar moments,
boxcars of dualities in the everyday

choices that we make. I have been
delivered, blessed by this guitar

that brought me home from forty years
in the urban American deserts,

back to the piney woods of Carolina,
this old rugged guitar, my cross

to bear, this everlasting church
of the mule-driving sharecroppers.

# ON THE ROAD TO BLESSING

Coming across Lake Pontchartrain
flying in my Aerostar after Katrina
the fall breaks past the mud of Slidell
then on the bridge barely above
the water through Bayou Sauvage
towards Chalmette and in the fog
the lights of the refinery a distant
glow of the lit towers and rigs
in the poverty of a starless night
give a false skyline a mirage of a city
the big oil money magic the temple
of Mammon only a slick smear
before I can get to New Orleans

# BEFORE THE BARS OPEN

At the Goodwill in Lauderdale
we found ourselves in front

of a huge bin of naked doll babies
and I asked my shipmates what year

did they put these Stripper Barbies
on the shelves, and after a moment

Rim-Rim-Sa-Sa-True-Sa said it must
have been before his twin daughters

were born and he was glad to not
see a brown doll in such a sad pile.

# BEFORE THE BARS CLOSE

Leaving Lauderdale we drove south, sailors
heading for the longer drinking hours

in the dives that mark the trail to Miami,
putting the spurs to our rented Mustang.

Keeping one hour ahead of the closings,
our wads of hazardous duty pay in the trunk,

the drinking money in our pockets.
Except, Mike who liked flashing

his entire country boy roll for those
sweet / surly girls in the sawdust bars.

# IN THE BAR

In the Liberty City section of Miami after
40 days underwater, here come the sailors,

and we submerge ourselves in beer and booze
in a bar that is named The Bar. We slapped

money in the jukebox and let the music
crash against us Gap Banding ourselves

with the local women. We get a plate of Caribbean
chicken wings and buy a fifth of whiskey

from the bar. Mike gets drunk, tells a brown girl
submariners do it deeper, he likes going down.

# AFTER THE BAR CLOSES

In the Mustang after doing concentric circles
through Liberty City after the girl

returned to the bar without Mike a half-hour
after they'd left, his piney woods laugh

grabbing her ass throwing an extra five dollars
on the cash stacked on the bar, her eyes

hungry brown on his pants, and now she's back
without him, our drunk crazy redneck friend and

that's when Rim-Rim asks her how she feels about
having party, taking a ride, getting high.

## WHAT HAPPENS IN THE MUSTANG
## STAYS IN THE MUSTANG

I start the pony, throw it in gear and peal off.
Rim-Rim climbs in the back with the girl

and asks her name and she immediately ups
the ante on the game, then she sees the blade

in Rim-Rim's hand. Take your clothes off, to her,
and tells me to shut up, I scream the fuck no.

Every piece she takes off, thrown out the window,
birds in the breeze. Knife tip in the thin

orbital bone above the eye. She shows us where
we find Mike stumbling in a shaming sunrise:

Rim-Rim tells me pull over, tells her good-bye.

# I TOLD YOU

Her voice was an earwig in my head
over and over a constant cerebral crawl
*I told you you cannot trust Jake*
who I'd lent the 100 dollars that I could
be taking her out to dinner with
and we're sitting here with me waiting
for Jake to call and I trust Jake but I know
it's a shame when you can't trust
the people you should be able to trust
like when somebody dies isn't there always
someone in the family overcome with greed
and you don't see it until the strike
has been made because who knew that crows
can weep like the rest of us who knew
a crow could cry crocodile tears
isn't there always someone who has stashed
all the jewelry taken the credit cards and all
the trees off the land of the dead person
isn't there always someone who leaves
us barren so they can wear a garment
made of scraps of scripture and bits
of cash isn't there always someone slick
and can't be trusted but I trust Jake
because I know he delivers
like he the last living bluesman
but I told him please be on time.

### The Bushman's Medicine Show

*My fetishes: prayers to god, hand-made*
*from whatever was near: a bluejay*
*feather, a shiny black stone,*
*a twisted knot of sassafras root,*
*two packets of the sacred dirt*
*from my grandmothers' graves*
*wrapped in the red from the flag*
*and dangling off my rearview mirror.*

# A TUESDAY IN THE CRACK WAR OF '97

## 1. Having Birthed a Holding Charge

*for Charles Bukowski*

Sitting on
his steel bunk
a homeless
dude been here
a month and
he's got crabs
so bad he
is now called
Baltimore
and was picked
up passed out
public drunk
laying on
the sidewalk
with a crack
pipe in his
shirt pocket
waiting for
him to flip
it he can't
understand
why he's here
since cocaine
residue
ain't like you
are still in
possession.

## 2. Going Solo

Ain't nobody seen him since
he got shot, grazed cross the shoulder,

hit in the foot. First the motherfucker took
his jacket so he wouldn't bleed on it.

His boys on the opposite corner
watched the rip-off going down without

even telling him they saw it coming.
He must have done something,

smoked the dope or stole a stash,
that they let him take that shit

without one of them lifting a gun-hand.
And now nobody knows where he is

but the whole block knows
what's on his mind.

### 3. Junieboy's Forty-Five:

gangland blue finish
clean with slick action
smelling of gun oil
and the credibility chamber
is loaded the hammer
half-cocked safety
eight Nato rounds
in the nine-round clip
cooling the passenger seat

## 4. Black Flag

Heat was dancing off Florida Avenue
around Fourth Street. In the traffic fumes
at the stoplight, he leans a braided head
out of his trunk, and sweating beneath
his shades, mouth full of tombstones
he says, Look on my truck seat and
check this: I bought this pound of cheese
a little while ago and I ran into a gal and
we went, everything tight, right, quick.
I didn't waste any time getting it done
and this cheese is already cooking
down to grease, and it's hot like
it was when them two little boys
were left in that rusted-out car last week,
they played until they got sluggish,
laid down in the back. The most mercy
I could show that rockhead mother,
who put them there and let them die,
is set her ass on fire in the middle
of whatever crackhouse she was in.

## 5. Fish Bait

Prison cafeteria: a muscle-neck
convict, a rogue double-wide in a row
of shotgun houses, cuts the line, slides up
behind the new boy and starts whispering
loud enough for those close by to witness
the drop and drag of the criminal hook;
first, that he hates so-called freedom fighters
and that here in this honor grade jailhouse
he fancies boys who haven't yet started
to shave, how amazingly fortunate
it is that the fish happened to be both
because the only thing he liked more than
kicking shit out of the so-called comrades
is putting the grease to a smooth face boy.

### 6. Penitent at 2 AM in the Holding Cell

Why shouldn't I be forgiven, being
that both sides of my family
are long half-lines of the Pentecost.
Most of the family men been reluctant,
bare knuckle congregants who only found
their shade of religion in jails,
or coming off a bender and seeing
the Gideon's Bible on the dresser
in some cinder block motel.
The women take after my sanctified
grandmothers and my great-aunts,
who had been pious white-dress-wearing
sisters of the low ground, who brought
the holy ghost and field hand songs
to everyone who crossed their paths.
So, why shouldn't some of that
good faith credit come to me,
considering that I have not done
any kind of sinning terribly wrong.

### The Bushman's Medicine Show

*The water we drink has been blessed,*
*but we have spent hundreds of years*
*under the accumulation of false facts,*
*a rot to the magic of the ancestor tree.*
*I have what you need for the proper*
*offerings, links of iron chain,*
*fresh tangerines, hand-rolled*
*Cubano cigars and silver crosses.*

# MEET ME IN THE BOTTOM

It is Friday night, the first in months
that I don't have to work, a janitor
in the long rooms of small cubicles
but I don't take trash from anybody.

I am the politely unseen.

Despite blackwater fishing, pies in the stove
and barbeque, North Carolina is the postcard
that you hobo out of. And so tonight
my buddy Chris and I sing trance blues,
hillbilly black gospel and Woody Guthrie songs.

November is nothing but the promise of snow.

We are blued, tattooed, and neither of us
lately have been regular church goers
or drinkers, but here we are: Maker's Mark,
a spirit in a jar, our holy water, our holy war.

Behold the blessed laborers looking for jobs.

Troubles: an old man, a Vietnam vet, got shot
by a young drug-addicted girl; bored cops
are dangerous, stay off the roads. I wonder how
bad it was before the devil was contained.

Nobody here rides easy, guitar in hand.

Carolina is no warm spot in the winter.
We are the uninsured low waged who
are not-to-be-messed-with tonight, we are
booze and rebellion music in the static.

Take Carolina and give it to the crows.

The streets are sheets of ice. We huddle
in front of the space heater, water pipes
are bursting all over Winston. I need to leave
thin streams flowing from all the faucets.

I need to get the cold out of my bones.

# THE WOOD

I swung a brand new eight-pound
splitting maul into a cross section
of trunk from an old cherry tree
with heart disease that had long
stopped bearing fruit, and it was hell
busting that cherry into stove wood,
fruit trees are more work
than all the other blessed trees,
like let's say the madrone, because,
if it ain't too green, madrone splits
with the smack of the maul as cleanly
as you cut a deck of cards, but this
was cherry and the maul's handle
splintered from the head down
to the knob and stung my hands
like I had slapped that cherry myself,
and I was embarrassed to take the maul
back to the hardware and appear that I
had used it wrong when the problem
was the wood had been machined
against the grain, so I got wood glue
and drilled holes, drove wood screws
up the handle, taped it like an optimist
with a broken baseball bat, but nothing
worked, so I go back to the store
and get another eight-pound maul,
but with a fiberglass handle
this time, and that's the maul
I am still using today and it does
satisfy my labor but there is some
residue, because when harvesting
wood for a handle for the maul

and for that axe now replaced
by a small noisy chainsaw
sounding like a curse near
the woodshed, there is some
disappointment to find even one
more of my innocuous rural
memory now tainted by this
damn sweat-less industrial
weakening of traditions.

## DOMESTIC VIOLENCE

Friday night and my neighbors are at it again,
their weekly ritual of rage and discontent.
She has speed dialed the law, and now
the scowling police are hand-on-gun
in the driveway of their ragged house
with loose nails and busted boards.
You can tell from their cautious walk
that the police hate this place, this man
and this woman, who I suppose at times
still love each other. I have seen them smile,
but not on the Fridays of the fried fish
and paycheck drama. The grass in the yard
is waist high and the house has a colony
of vermin that the man and woman
wage war on every day but Friday.
Rats are behind the walls, scurrying back and
forth in the stricken pace of the spasms
that come with digesting poisons: their soft
innards deteriorating, the desperate hearts
beating themselves to death. The two
police cars are parked on the wrong side
of the street, facing the flow of one-way traffic,
their red and blue lights are the rain storm
against my neighbors' windows. He is sober,
and in the tall yard he compliantly turns
for the customary bracelets and the waiting
in jail come Monday morning to see the magistrate.
There are no tables busted, no overturned
stewpot, there is not a mark on her as she stands
barefoot in the cold yard and curse-testifies
before the neighborhood on his alleged assault.

# WHEN MY FIRST WIFE LEFT ME

I should have seen the signs,
should have seen it coming
when she proclaimed my heartbeat
was like some far off shit nobody hears
but other dogs like me. I was raised
never to say such a thing or ask
what called her to me so I won't
but I will say she is one badass
perpetual scowl. She likes to fight,
she likes having make-up sex,
an argument, a shot of whiskey,
and then the charge. I ain't got no
problem with that, no complaints,
and that my friends, yes, even you
sorry-ass drinkers of vodka can be
my friends tonight if you don't talk
so I won't have to smell it on your breath,
my not complaining was the problem.
It meant she had to create all the reasons
for whatever fighting we did. Always
pushing and pulling on me like that
was some type of domestic agreement,
and she got mad at me not getting mad.
I was raised different in Cackalack,
I've breakfasted with moonshine whiskey
and government grits. I should
have read the signs. Don't know
why she think she so dignified?
My grandmothers, my mother
and all my aunts conjure, mystics
of the hollers, proud folk ,mine,
and her people, just a razor cut

above squalor, and her father
who once drew his rusty revolver
on me, is from a long obese line
of snake-handling goat fuckers.

# DRIVING AT NIGHT TOWARDS
# THE HOOD CANAL

Even when I am not
speeding I get stopped
for speeding and there

is no room for a question
to a cop positioning his
shooting stance outside

my rolled down window
in the dangerous wash
of red and blue lights

the Dirty Harry Dixie
a murder soundtrack
we both know is playing

and there is no protest from
or protection for me there is
the skim of this moment

that thin layer of skin
covering the whole situation
there is only the space

of a breath between
what should happen
and what could happen

# ARS POETICA

One thing I can tell you about this drinking hole that is always thick with stumbling writers is that if there are no seats they will fall and sit on the floor. And everybody knows the old novelist who won a lying contest by telling a bold truth about himself. There are shape shifters in here who are not afraid to break a bone or swallow a tooth or two. Even the quiet writers will sometimes throw a table through the window just to watch the reaction and other writers will gather the shards and slivers like they're precious stones. And they will still be served because the bartender is also a writer who knows they drink good whiskeys and generally give great anecdotal tips. You never know what or who is going to stir things up, but when the hoodoo woman in her blue cotton dress zydeco-ed a prose poem on the mahogany bar the men and the women poets with tattoos all wanted her. They came to their alligator-shoed feet like happy hour hurricanes were going two for the price of one, smoothing out their last wrinkled dollars and pushing them into that hungry neon juke. They were reaching and calling out, falling over themselves to dance with her. Absolutely a poet should have this type of desperate desire, and a clean shot of predicted hardship: knowing any moment could get hot and southern humid as an unfinished hankering song, and then they'll have to get past that dog in her yard, that off-the-chain inadequacy of words.

## SIMMER DOWN

Take the peace-be-still bath
when feeling over-amped
from the sustained intensity
of spirits in your proximity,
or when feeling overwhelmed
by your earthly conditions.
Gather a peck of lavender,
most effective when in bloom

and the sun and moon give it
daily blessings, the flowers,
when dried, even, provide
an aromatic testament to that.
Pick an armful of magnolia
blossoms and leaves for the mix.
For this ritual engage only what is
beautiful in the dirty South.

Add a handful of sprigs, the soft
needles from the tips of the branches
of an evergreen. Bundle four stalks
of lavender with purple cloth for the altar
that must be placed near the bath.
Use very hot water, pour in the mix
and let it steep until the bath cools
enough to comfortably enter.

As the bath steeps, at the altar
burn frankincense and myrrh,
and light the multi-colored candle
for the Seven African Powers,
who through Oyá will soothe you

and drive away the Disturbs,
those frantic shoulder-riding spirits
that place confusion in the mind.

During the bath the entire body
must be soaked, wash the head
and proceed down, let stress and
doubts flow from you: the torso,
particularly from the heart which
is tired and needs relief, the arms
and hands, to the legs, feet and toes,
and then let your best self step out.

## The Bushman's Medicine Show

*Praise whatever done to have you here,*
*a god promise received at night, maybe*
*a solitary flickering white candle*
*with a drop of lavender oil to sweeten*
*the air for song, go to the barn,*
*I got blues stacked by the bushels.*
*Let me put some light on your head,*
*an old gray fedora, comfortable, warm,*
*softly pinched and styled in belief*
*that with god word is bond.*

# WHY I DON'T BELIEVE IN LEVEES

I can no longer trust the levees
and I want to believe in God
but I've been down to New Orleans
so I truly believe in flood
  and the ghost of the lower 9th ward
Most the homes been washed away
not one stray dog on the street
muddy flowers in the graveyard
pleasure boats ride the trees
  I been searching for my God
  and found this unholy flood
The churches were under water
and no one was getting baptized
all the saints they were drowning
when the gators came to town
  I been down in New Orleans
  cleaning prayers from the flood
I seen so much water destruction
the devastation to all those souls
two thousand people still are missing
drag the river for their bones O God
drag the river for the bones

# ASHEVILLE

Homeless angels sing in the city
in the mountain hollers and evergreens
North Carolina land of the slave
drive Highway 40 through the home of the brave
Thomas Wolfe and O. Henry but
ain't no monuments for anybody Cherokee
        except at the cigar store

Well, let me stop and catch my breath
gotta cut out smoking these cigarettes
and dropping the butts in Asheville

Screw the popguns damn the magnums
and the hollow-point loaded American canon
I got dog-eared pages of Jean Toomer
the whole revolution the Black Arts Movement
I mix them together and work it like a potion
so come on now put me to the test
and I'll bust a poem
to my last cigarette
down Highway 40 off the bypass
low hourly wage at the textile mill

Three hundred miles from my family
ain't none of us crazy
handling snakes
the misdemeanors and the felonies
teachers hustlers lawyers and ministers
this colorful weave of saints and sinners
gets together on the holidays

and drink and smoke
and deal the cards Jesus saves
a backwoods church and cemetery
libations at the graves of our ancestors

# THE BONEYARD

Yes, our dead will have us, always.
So I call on the spirits, everything
is proper under the 200-year-old oak

that lost its top when that heavy rain
and wind rolled in summer before last.
Still, on the hot days that tree throws

plenty of shade on my people
in the cemetery at Riddick Grove,
and when the weather's good I play

my djembe for them. I knock
on the door, the rhythm. I ring the bell.
Uncle Bear smokes so I leave a cigar

by his tombstone; his children
all gone North so I do it for them:
the four daughters, the son, love him,

there is no past tense. I will keep
this line of graves free of weeds,
and being a man without children

I pray someone comes to read a poem
in the boneyard for me, someone
splashing bourbon like a gospel song.

# ISAAC IN THE SHADOW OF ABRAHAM

Maybe, he was beaten first,
his father drunk with god
calling for sacrifice,
the blooding of the altar.
Maybe they had never
gotten along and it was
an issue of paternity,
the bloodied butcher knife.
The familial hand holding
the blade against his throat,
the keen edge, the thinnest line
of blood. Can you understand
I don't believe he went
without a fuss to that altar,
because if he did why would
Abraham, his sainted father,
have had to bind him?

# FOR PEACE IN THE VALLEY

To ward off street violence, at midnight
perform the ritual on the corner, in the cross,
hustlers, most likely, will be watching,

cleanse yourself before you start: bathe, put on
fresh garments, white or as close as you can get,
nothing dark, tell the hustlers what you are doing.

In the intersection draw a Vévé for Papa Legba
with white chalk, leave a bit of red cloth, a red flower,
sacrifice has already been made, do not wash away

any blood that may remain in the street.
Near the oak tree where the boys stand, where
they have been dying, place a glass of gin

(white rum, or moonshine), a lit candle, either red
or white; light a cigar, blow the smoke to the Vévé,
then leave it burning beside the other offerings.

On the corner, read aloud and place the 23rd Psalm
(do not tear it from the Holy Bible) then smash
a coconut at the Vévé leaving all the shards

in the intersection, spray from a bottle of gin
in the four directions of the cross, ask Papa Legba
to end the shootings, the hustlers are watching.

# LOVE POEM: WE BOTH DRINK, SOMETIMES

more than we need and dance into our glasses not caring so
much to the what to the when to the who and why except that
now you have made room in your heart and bed for me sliding
it from against the wall both loosening and capturing me with
the open space and we get up different in our mornings mine
a soft strummed guitar the approaching light the porch and
remembering how we curled into the body of each other and laid
close to the embers of that fire the hard love that whiskey does
not change and these same mornings have seen you stretched
corner to corner across the heated bed until near noon and
usually under the covers except that one morning you asked
me to never talk about again when you were naked and exposed
and beautiful in the light and so utterly comfortable under the
open window a breeze of northwest cool coming through and
you blessed by your warrior-witch spirits from the bottle of the
night before remember love remember how we drank like that.

# MY SISTER'S RAY-BANS

*In memory of Cynthia Vanessa Lilley Hargis*

When I put these shades on I am seeing
North Beach through her glasses; a loaded
freighter heading out, slowly distancing me,

about an hour in front of the line where water
meets sky; a powerboat cuts a tail, its bow
bouncing high off the water and I am grateful

its obnoxious whine quickly fades in the wind.
The Whidbey Island cliffs, across the Sound,
before they blend into the Cascade Mountains,

are steep, and a righteous vantage is established
in the perspective of smallness in the huge Douglas firs
that I know tops their crowns.

Off the point where leaning trees struggle
out of stone, the sunset puts a broad beam
across the water, towards the rocky beach.

The lone squawk of a gull is the blue-note
underneath the persistent slosh of the tide,
the relentless waves giving and taking away.

# A PROPER ELEGY FOR MY FATHER

He is the black Marlboro man, the oldest son of a one-legged gold-tooth rounder. Abandoned homes down the road have fallen into ruin. Everything dies hard here, collapses into the kudzu pulling it down. This is the low-ground, the land of the Maroons from the Great Dismal Swamp. Nothing lasts forever. The honeysuckle from the ditch-bank, and from the woods behind the house, is in the air tonight, with the croaking of frogs and the waxing moon. A soft touch of southern intoxication and I almost don't want to light my cigarette, but I do. This is North Carolina, the tobacco state, even though most farmers nowadays are paid to not grow it. Here, traditions die hard. Out of the fog plantation ghosts and Jim Crow walk tall, persistent as the oppressive kudzu, as old as the Dixie lost cause. We are born into this, and if we are lucky our fathers prepare us to live in it. Show us how to stand and throw down. Food for the table: they teach us to fish and hunt, to enjoy setting the hook, the recoil of the shotgun, the striking of the target. The rural cycle of life, everything dies hard here. Except my father: a scowl and a growl, a piney woods drawl, a drinker of dirty water, a two-fisted church deacon, a logwood man, a long haul truck-driving Korean War veteran whose face was set so serene in his coffin that it was evident he'd died in his sleep. Unafraid as death approached, he'd said he was going to take a nap. His thick-fingered friends: a gathering of old crows weeping into their handkerchiefs at the wake. I say to myself, look at him, old-black-man-cool in the blue suit that he will wear forever. Who doesn't want to die like that, nothing coming down the road but rest.